# Gigi's Great Adventures

## by Gina Marie Angelini

AuthorHouse™
1663 Liberty Drive
Bloomington, IN 47403
www.authorhouse.com
Phone: 1 (800) 839-8640

Published by AuthorHouse 03/08/2019

ISBN: 978-1-5462-7600-5 (sc)
ISBN: 978-1-5462-7601-2 (hc)
ISBN: 978-1-5462-7599-2 (e)

Library of Congress Control Number: 2019900842

Print information available on the last page.

This book is printed on acid-free paper.

authorHOUSE®

My dedication goes out to my husband Gerry, who I have been happily married to for 15 blessed years. His encouragement means the world to me.

Also, to my beautiful sister Tara and little Sammy that inspired me to write about a dog.

One more person is my kindhearted friend Cathy, who gave me the confidence to write my very first book.

To the rest of my family & friends, I am hopeful there will be a sequel.

Stay tuned.


Thank you,

Gina Marie

Hello! My name is Gigi.

The very first place I would love to visit is the Caribbean Island, Jamaica. It is so wonderful to be swimming in the crystal blue ocean. I'm excited to go snorkeling for the first time.

Wow! Look at those brightly colored fish! There is even a crab and a stingray swimming by with a turtle.

She is now feeling the sand between her paws, and smells some jerk chicken near by the beach.

A man greets her and says "Hello, mon!"

"Would you like to try our famous jerk chicken today?"

"Yes, please! And some coconut water also, thank you."

The next country she visited was Italy, where she went on a fascinating ride down the canals on a gondola.

She saw brightly colored and charming tall buildings with stunning landscapes all around them.

She also got to go under a beautiful unique bridge with stone arches.

After such a delightful ride, she looked around for an Italian restaurant.

She sees one and goes in and is greeted by a man "Ciao, madam…"

"Where would you like to be seated?"

She says, "By the window please."

She is very impressed by the atmosphere of the restaurant, with the delightful flower arrangement on her table and music playing above her.

The spaghetti and meatballs are absolutely delicious and just what she was craving.

Still in Italy, she went to visit the Angel's Zoo.

With all the amazing animals, she stopped to see the bird section. First, the stunning owl with powerful yellow eyes! The second cage she saw had a gorgeous bald eagle with a golden beak. And she saw an ostrich with a long neck!

As she was admiring all the impressive animals, she saw an extra-large cage with a massive brown bear with giant claws. He was fantastic.

In the last two cages she saw a red fox, which was adorable, and a raccoon with her miniature babies that looked so snuggly and warm next to their mama.

ANGELS ZOO

Gigi is now waking up from her long incredible nap.

The sound of water is trickling down a stream as she looks over and sees a duck and four babies following behind her.

She can smell the popcorn popping in the distance...

# The End

Printed in the United States
By Bookmasters